PHOTOS FRAMED

A FRESH LOOK AT THE WORLD'S MOST MEMORABLE PHOTOGRAPHS

RUTH THOMSON

CANDLEWICK PRESS

The author would like to thank the following people for their help with this book:
Virginia Chandler, John Kenward, Brigitte Lardinois, Gilly Lacey, Caroline Pic, and Chloë Thomson.

Photo credits: William Anders/NASA: 20 detail, 21; Ansel Adams Publishing Rights Trust/Corbis: 18 detail, 19; Cecil Beaton/IWM/Getty Images: 42 detail, 43; Jean-Baptiste Sabatier-Blot/wikimedia: 4 detail, 5; Hugo Burnand; All rights reserved by the British Monarchy: 12 detail, 13; Stephen Dalton/Nature PL: 26 detail, 27; Robert Doisneau/Gamma-Rapho/Getty Images: 44 detail, 45; Charles C. Ebbets/Bettmann/Corbis: 38 detail, 39; emran/Shutterstock: front cover; Elliott Erwitt/Magnum Photos: 50 detail, 51; Georg Gerster/Panos Pictures: 22 detail, 23; Andreas Gursky/G Bild-Kunst/DACS 2013 Courtesy Sprüth Magers Berlin London: 34 detail, 35; David Hockney: 32 detail, 33; Korda/Alamy: 8 detail, 9; Dorothea Lange/Corbis: 40 detail, 41; Neil Leifer/Sports Illustrated/Getty Images: 46 detail, 47; Steve McCurry/Magnum Photos: 10 detail, 11; Gjon Mili/TimeLife Pictures/Getty Images: 6 detail, 7; Eadweard Muybridge/Corbis: 16 detail, 17; NASA: 48 detail, 49; Martin Parr/Magnum Photos: 56 detail, 57; Oskana Perkins/Shutterstock: 2 bottom; Cristina Garcia Rodero/Magnum Photos: 14 detail, 15; Sebastião Selgado/Amazonas Images/*nbpictures: 52 detail, 53; Vasily Smirnov/Shutterstock: 3; Thomas Struth: 24 detail, 25; Ruth Thomson: 2 top; The Warhol Foundation/Superstock: 30 detail, 31; Jeff Widener/AP/PAI: 54 detail, 55; Elsie Wright/Topfoto: 36 detail, 37.

Every attempt has been made to clear copyright. Should there be any inadvertent omission, please apply to the publisher for rectification.

First U.S. edition 2014

Library of Congress Catalog Card Number pending
ISBN 978-0-7636-7154-9

14 15 16 17 18 19 TOM 10 9 8 7 6 5 4 3 2 1

Printed in Shah Alam, Selangor, Malaysia

This book was typeset in Frutiger and DIN OT.

Candlewick Press
99 Dover Street
Somerville, Massachusetts 02144

visit us at www.candlewick.com

How to Read This Book

Photos Framed encourages you, the reader, to engage directly with the included photographs. When the text asks questions or discusses visual details, you're invited to look closely at the image before moving on to the next part of the text. The book was designed to help you give each photograph your full consideration, requiring you to rotate the book for photographs shot in a landscape orientation. (While you do so, you might think about how photos in portrait orientation—taller than wide—and landscape orientation—wider than tall—both showcase their subjects.)

Contents

Introduction

Portrait photography

Louis Daguerre, by Jean-Baptiste Sabatier-Blot   4

Pablo Picasso, by Gjon Mili   6

Heroic Guerrilla Fighter, by Alberto Korda   8

Afghan Girl, by Steve McCurry   10

Royal Wedding, by Hugo Burnand   12

Meily Mendoza Singing to Her Doll, by Cristina Garcia Rodero   14

Nature photography

The Horse in Motion, by Eadweard Muybridge   16

The Tetons and the Snake River, by Ansel Adams   18

Earthrise, by William Anders   20

Camel Caravan, by Georg Gerster   22

Sunflower No. 4, by Thomas Struth   24

Ladybird Take-off, by Stephen Dalton   26

Photography as art

Io + Gatto (I + Cat), by Wanda Wulz   28

Marilyn Diptych, by Andy Warhol   30

Pearblossom Highway #2, by David Hockney   32

99 Cent, by Andreas Gursky   34

Documentary photography

The Cottingley Fairies, by Elsie Wright   36

Lunchtime atop a Skyscraper, by Charles C. Ebbets   38

Migrant Mother, by Dorothea Lange   40

Air-Raid Victim, London Blitz, by Cecil Beaton   42

The Kiss by the Hôtel de Ville, by Robert Doisneau   44

Muhammad Ali versus Sonny Liston, by Neil Leifer   46

Buzz Aldrin on the Moon, by Neil Armstrong   48

New York City, by Elliott Erwitt   50

Serra Pelada Gold Mine, by Sebastião Salgado   52

Tank Man, by Jeff Widener   54

Barcelona, by Martin Parr   56

Glossary   58

Index   61

ntroduction

About this book

When photography began, it was an elaborate, expensive, time-consuming, elite activity, using heavy, cumbersome equipment. Today, taking photographs can be instant, cheap, and accessible to anyone. Despite the enormous changes in photographic equipment and technology since the nineteenth century, the purposes of photography have remained essentially the same, whether immortalizing, exploring, documenting, revealing, or showing us what we can't see with the naked eye.

Divided by themes, this book tells the stories behind some memorable photographs spanning the history of photography, chosen for the vividness or importance of their subject matter, their pioneering photographic technique, or their historic significance.

Portrait photography

Before photography was invented, portraits were drawn or painted and only the very rich could afford them. Early portrait photographers often copied the styles of painted portraits, posing ordinary people wearing their best clothes in front of backdrops painted with columns and drapes to add a sense of grandeur.

Good portraits reveal something about a person's personality or mood. Close-ups (pp. 9 and 11) are the most intimate and personal. Wider shots (p. 7) include an environment that suggests a sense of someone's life or work. Group portraits (p. 13) celebrate special or formal occasions when people come together.

Nature photography

Dramatic landscapes and weather, wildlife behavior and habitats, and the beauty and growth of plants are the main subjects of nature photography. Nature photographers emphasize the marvels of the natural world, often using specialized equipment to freeze motion (pp. 17 and 27), show a close-up view (p. 25), show the view from a long distance (p. 19), or take an unusual perspective (p. 23).

Photography as art

People have long claimed that photography is an artistic discipline in its own right, which people can enjoy for aesthetic pleasure. Today, the works of many contemporary photographers hang alongside paintings in art galleries and museums and are sold at high prices in auctions, just like other fine art. Several fine artists, including Andy Warhol and David Hockney, have made artworks (pp. 31 and 33) using photography.

Documentary photography

Images that provide visual evidence of particular cultural, political, or environmental situations or events are called documentary photographs. Many documentary photographers work on long-term stories about specific groups of people, including refugees, remote communities, tourists (p. 57), workers (pp. 39 and 53), the rural poor (p. 41), and those in wartime (p. 43). Their images are often shocking, attracting public attention and empathy. Other photographers roam cities and shoot otherwise overlooked details of daily life (p. 51). Photojournalists usually work on specific assignments for newspapers and magazines, capturing key visual moments of news events (pp. 47 and 55).

Photography as truth?

It has been said that "the camera never lies," but this is not so. *The Cottingley Fairies* (p. 37) is a famous example of a hoax photograph, and Doisneau's apparently documentary picture (p. 45) was, in fact, staged. All photographs are selected and framed frozen moments that ignore everything beyond the frame. Photographers have often cropped a photograph for heightened effect (p. 9). Sometimes, they intensify tones or combine two negatives together (p. 29). Today, it is also possible to manipulate photographs using sophisticated computer programs.

Photo thoughts

- 📷 What is the main focus of each photograph in the book?
- 📷 What might have been left out of the image?
- 📷 Which of the photos makes the greatest impression on you? Can you think why?

Louis Daguerre 1844

Jean-Baptiste Sabatier-Blot (French, 1801–1881)

The photograph

This is a portrait of Louis Daguerre, who produced the first permanent photographs, which were called daguerreotypes after their inventor. He announced his achievement to the French Academy of Sciences in 1839. The French government was so impressed that it gave Daguerre a lifetime pension in exchange for the rights to his invention. Daguerreotypes became very popular, especially in America. Sealed with glass to prevent them from tarnishing, the images were framed and kept in velvet-lined leather cases.

Daguerreotypes needed a long exposure and lots of light. Studios had glass roofs to let in as much light as possible. Daguerre would have felt very hot sitting with sunlight shining directly onto his face. His head, neck, and back were probably held in braces, so that he could keep perfectly still for the minutes-long exposure.

The photographer

To make a daguerreotype, the photographer cleaned and buffed a silver-coated copper plate until it gleamed. He or she then sensitized the plate with chemicals before putting it in the camera. When the photographer took off the camera's lens cap, the plate was exposed to light. After the plate was developed over warm mercury vapor, an image appeared. It was fixed (stabilized) with salt water. Each daguerreotype was a unique, fragile, reflective image.

Photo thoughts

- 📷 What impression do you think Daguerre wanted to create with his portrait?
- 📷 Why were images like this considered precious?
- 📷 When photography was invented, artists feared this would be the end of portrait painting. Do you think this has happened?

Blow Up

Why do you think Daguerre's right hand is clenched into a fist?

Zoom In ▶

Daguerre wears the clothes of a fashionable man: a dark suit with big buttons, a satin vest, a high collar, and a cravat. His pose, with an elbow resting on a table, copies the pose of wealthy people in portrait paintings of his time.

Jean-Baptiste Sabatier-Blot/wikimedia

"I have seized the light. I have arrested its flight." — Louis Daguerre

Pablo Picasso 1949

Gjon Mili (Albanian-American, 1904–1984)

Blow Up

Picasso drew the Minotaur with a single unbroken line. How did he draw its eyes?

The photograph

Mili was given an assignment by *Life* magazine to visit Picasso, the famous Spanish artist, in the south of France. He showed Picasso his photos of ice skaters leaping in the dark with minute lights fixed to their skates. These gave Picasso an idea. Using a small electric light in a darkened room, the artist quickly drew the swirling outline of a Minotaur—half bull, half man—in the air. Of course, this fleeting work of art disappeared almost as soon as it was made, but Mili captured it on film for posterity. He was able to capture the entire movement of Picasso's light drawing by using a very slow shutter speed (the time that the shutter remains open).

The photographer

Originally trained as an electrical engineer, Mili was a self-taught photographer. Renowned for his innovations with strobe lighting and long exposures, he specialized in capturing a sequence of actions in a single photo, making time appear frozen. He used this technique to make studies of moving dancers, athletes, musicians, and skaters.

Photo thoughts

 Is the Minotaur drawing a Picasso artwork, even if it exists only as a photograph?

 What words would you use to describe Picasso from looking at this photograph?

 What movements did Picasso make with his body to create this image?

Zoom In ▶

The plates and dishes on the shelves and the jugs on the floor were all painted by Picasso. He created a huge number of ceramics while living in the pottery town of Vallauris between 1948 and 1955.

*"*To draw, you must close your eyes and sing.*"*

— Pablo Picasso

Heroic Guerrilla Fighter 1960

Alberto Díaz Gutiérrez (known as Korda) (Cuban, 1928–2001)

The photograph

Argentinian-born Che Guevara was a charismatic guerrilla commander in the Cuban revolution and a key member of the new Cuban government. This picture of him was hurriedly snapped at a state funeral for Cubans killed in a freighter explosion in Havana's harbor. The image has since become a potent symbol of resistance and radical protest movements. Converted into a simplified black-and-white graphic, Che's face has also been hijacked for commercial purposes, reproduced on countless posters, T-shirts, postcards, mugs, and advertisements.

The photographer

Korda was Cuba's top fashion photographer until the Cuban revolution in 1959. Then he became President Fidel Castro's personal photographer, recording Castro's activities in Cuba and abroad. His photographs were often published in the Cuban daily newspaper *Revolucíon*.

Photo thoughts

- 📷 Che's shoulders face one direction and his head faces another. What effect does this have?
- 📷 How does the contrast of light and dark give Che's face such a powerful presence?
- 📷 Why do you think this image has been reproduced so many times?

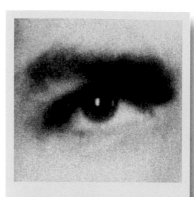

Blow Up

Che's eyes look upward, past the camera, toward a far horizon. How do you think he was feeling?

Zoom In ▶

Korda's original shot was landscape-shaped, showing Che's head and shoulders against an expanse of sky, with the profile of a man on Che's left and palm leaves on his right. Korda cropped the image very tightly, getting rid of the distracting elements, and reframed it into a portrait shape, with Che's head filling most of the image.

"This photograph is not the product of knowledge or technique. It was really coincidence, pure luck." —Alberto Korda

Afghan Girl 1985

Steve McCurry (American, b. 1950)

The photograph

With her piercing green eyes staring straight at us, this portrait of a twelve-year-old girl has come to symbolize the upheaval of people during war and the plight of refugees. The photographer, Steve McCurry, shot the image in a refugee camp on the Afghanistan-Pakistan border. It appeared on the cover of *National Geographic* magazine, accompanying an article about the refugees. McCurry didn't know the girl's name or what had happened to her until 2002. After a long search, McCurry and a TV crew discovered her back in her home village in Afghanistan. She was now a married woman with three daughters. Her name is Sharbat Gula.

The photographer

A celebrated photojournalist, McCurry has photographed wars in many countries as well as Afghanistan, including Iraq, Lebanon, Cambodia, and the Persian Gulf. On one of his earliest assignments in Afghanistan, he disguised himself in local garb and sewed rolls of film into his clothes to keep them safe.

Photo thoughts

 How does the girl's direct stare make you feel?

How might the effect of this photograph have differed if the photographer had taken a wider shot?

If you had to put this photograph into a category, which would you choose: portrait or documentary or both? Why?

Blow Up

What adjectives would you use to describe the girl's expression?

Zoom In ▶

Notice how the red of the girl's headscarf stands out against the green of the tent in the background and frames her face. Red and green are known as complementary colors. Placed side by side, they make each other seem brighter.

Steve McCurry/Magnum Photos

"This portrait summed up for me the trauma . . . of suddenly having to flee your home and end up in a refugee camp, hundreds of miles away." —Steve McCurry

Royal Wedding 2011

Hugo Burnand (British, b. 1963)

The photograph

This is an official photograph of the wedding of England's Prince William and Kate Middleton, showing the two families ranged on either side of the bride and groom.

The photographer had less than thirty minutes for the photo shoot, scheduled to occur between the wedding party's return from Westminster Abbey and their appearance on the balcony of Buckingham Palace. Burnand therefore had to plan the shoot carefully. He decided where everyone would be positioned and held a dress rehearsal in the grand throne room of the palace with staff standing in for the families. He placed the two chairs exactly where he wanted them and lit the room to give the effect of a fine spring morning.

The photographer

Hugo Burnand is an established portrait photographer. He had already taken the official photograph to mark Princes Charles's sixtieth birthday and the marriage photographs of Prince Charles to the Duchess of Cornwall. He was able to chat and joke with the families, putting everyone at ease, to create relaxed and friendly images.

Photo thoughts

- ◉ What does this image tell you about the two families?
- ◉ What do the colors and details of the setting contribute to the photograph?
- ◉ Compare this wedding photograph with those of your own family. What similarities and differences do you notice?

Blow Up

Do you think that the linked hands of the Duchess of Cornwall and her granddaughter were posed or spontaneous?

Zoom In ▶

Notice how the newly-wed couple stands out from their families, framed by the dark velvet canopy behind them. William's and Kate's arms are linked and lifted up to emphasize their togetherness.

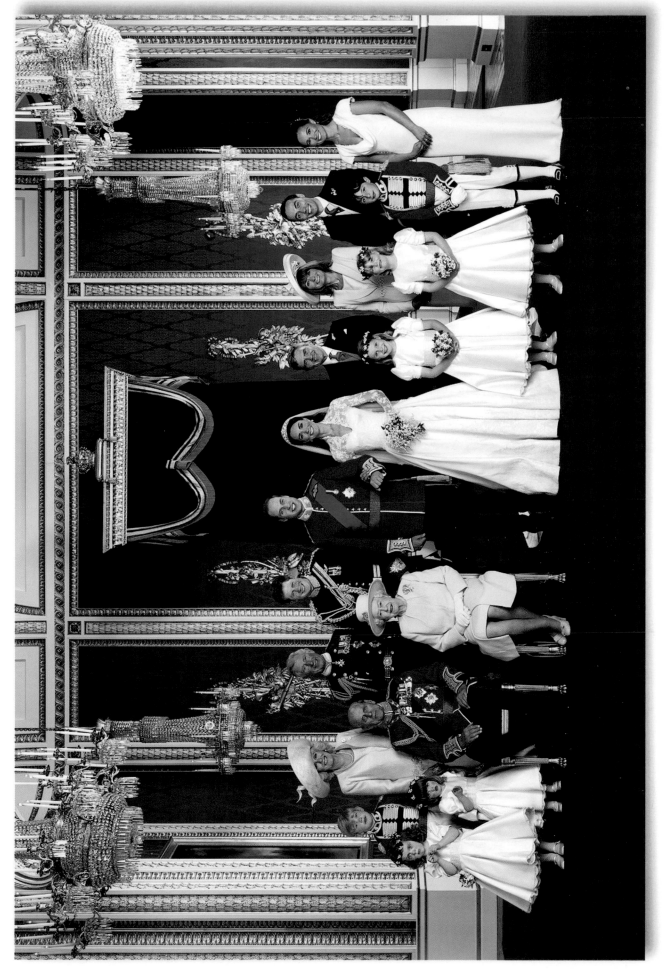

"From where I was, and from their point of view, it was two families coming together." —Hugo Burnand

Meily Mendoza Singing to Her Doll 2011

Cristina Garcia Rodero (Spanish, b. 1949)

The photograph

This intimate photograph of Meily Mendoza is one of the portraits that Rodero shot for a photo essay of Baracoa, an isolated city surrounded by mountains on the far eastern coast of Cuba. Her photographs commemorate the five hundredth anniversary of Baracoa, Cuba's oldest colonial settlement, founded by Spanish conquistadors in 1511. Meily seems totally unaware of the camera, singing lovingly to the doll she holds tightly in her arms. Strangely, the doll seems to look out at the viewer instead.

Rodero spent several weeks in Baracoa, documenting scenes of daily life in streets, shops, schools, homes, and fields, as well as taking a series of striking portraits.

The photographer

Rodero studied painting before she took up photography. She has specialized in documenting traditions, rituals, and festivities, both religious and secular, first in Spain, then in other parts of Europe, and more recently in Haiti. Wherever she travels, she spends considerable time with the people that she is going to photograph.

Photo thoughts

- 📷 Do you think Meily Mendoza posed for this photograph?
- 📷 Does it feel as if the photographer was "invisible" to Meily?
- 📷 What can you tell about the people of Baracoa from this portrait of Meily?

Blow Up

How does this photograph capture Meily's affection for her doll?

Zoom In ▶

This photograph is rich with textures and patterns. Meily stands in front of a roughly plastered wall. Her dress is decorated with lace and embroidery. Her doll wears a hat, dress, and shoes in matching flower-patterned fabric.

"I'm interested in people who are never going to make the news." —Cristina Garcia Rodero

The Horse in Motion 1878

Eadweard Muybridge (British, 1830–1904)

The photograph

Hoping to breed faster racehorses, Leland Stanford, a wealthy American racehorse owner, wanted to know whether a horse lifted all four hooves off the ground when it galloped. No one could see this with the naked eye. He hired Eadweard Muybridge, an English photographer, to discover the answer. Muybridge set up twenty-four glass-plate cameras in a line along a racetrack on Stanford's stock farm. The high-speed shutter on each camera was triggered by the horse's movement over trip wires.

The photographer

Muybridge had been a well-known landscape photographer in California. After taking this horse sequence, he spent several years taking thousands more pictures of animals and people in motion and compiled them into a book. Modern animators still use his book as a reference today. Muybridge toured the country showing his slides on a zoopraxiscope, a projection device he invented.

Photo thoughts

- Which of the photographs prove that all the horse's hooves lift off the ground?
- Are the frames in the sequence all different or are any identical?
- Muybridge first used twelve cameras to photograph a horse trotting, then set up twenty-four to capture the gallop. Why might he have done that?

Blow Up

Does the position of the rider change much in the sequence?

Zoom In ▶

Follow each of the horse's four legs in turn, to see how the front and back legs bend and stretch in relationship to one another. Notice when only the front or the back legs are on the ground.

© Eadweard Muybridge/Corbis

"The painter constructs, the photographer discloses."

—Susan Sontag, *On Photography*

The Tetons and the Snake River 1942

Ansel Adams (American, 1902–1984)

The photograph

Rocky mountains, rippling water, tree-covered land, and cloud-filled sky—in Adams's carefully framed image, all these elements of nature are in balance. They create a feeling of beauty, peace, and timelessness, untouched by human presence. By showing the river snaking from one side of the photograph to the other, Adams leads our eye through the landscape to the faraway mountains, just as if we were there.

Adams used a bulky, large-format camera. Using the smallest aperture and a slow shutter speed, he was able to achieve remarkable depth of field, meaning that the distant mountains are in just as sharp focus and detail as the foreground trees.

The photographer

Adams was a masterful photographer who shared his passion and expertise through writing, lectures, and hands-on workshops. He was also an environmentalist and used his photographs of the wilderness to persuade the United States government to preserve areas of natural beauty as national parks.

Photo thoughts

- Which parts of this picture are whitest and blackest? How many in-between shades of gray can you identify?
- What effect does the high angle of this image have on the way that you see it?
- Why do you think this picture was chosen as one of the 115 images sent aboard the *Voyager* spacecraft into outer space?

Blow Up

How does the sky help give the scene a sense of grandeur?

Zoom In ▶

By carefully controlling both the exposure and the development of the film, Adams was able to create a dramatic atmosphere. He ensured that the paler watery parts—river and snow—contrast very strongly with the dark foreground trees and the rocks.

"A good photograph is knowing where to stand." —Ansel Adams

Earthrise 1968

William Anders (American, b. 1933)

The photograph

Hailed as the most influential environmental photograph ever taken, this shot shows a view of the earth rising above the moon's surface. It was taken through the tiny window of a lunar module by William Anders, one of the three-person crew on the *Apollo 8* mission, the first manned voyage to orbit the moon. The astronauts' job was to take images of the moon's surface, including the far side (which can never be seen from Earth), scouting out possible landing spots for future missions. But this photograph may have done a far more important job, reminding people of the fragility and finite resources of our own planet.

The photographer

As flight engineer on the mission, Anders was tasked with testing all the systems for simulating a lunar landing. Frank Borman, the mission commander, took most of the photographs of the moon. It was only by chance that Anders glanced out of the window, spotted the earth appearing, and quickly snapped this powerful photograph.

Photo thoughts

📷 Why do you think this picture gave rise to the idea of "Spaceship Earth"?

📷 How does this picture of the earth make you feel?

📷 What caption would you give to this photograph?

Blow Up

The earth appears to be lying on its side from this view. Can you spot the west coast of Africa and the snow of Antarctica?

Zoom In ▶

The desolate, dead gray surface of the moon is pitted with craters, where comets and meteorites bombarded it in the long-distant past. There could hardly be a stronger contrast in color with the brilliant blues and swirling whites of the earth.

William Anders/NASA

"We came all this way to explore the Moon and the most important thing is that we discovered the Earth." —William Anders

Camel Caravan 1976

Georg Gerster (Swiss, b. 1928)

The photograph

Given special personal permission by the empress of Iran, Gerster took hundreds of aerial pictures of Iran, including this one of a camel caravan making its way along a sandy road. From this unusual high viewpoint, it is hard to identify the camels. However, the long shadows cast by their bodies make them instantly recognizable, despite their elongated, spindly legs. Their loads and riders are also revealed in silhouette. From this perspective, the human intervention of the road appears as a slash across the desert landscape.

Blow Up

What time of day do you think it was when Gerster took this photograph?

The photographer

Gerster has spent fifty years taking aerial photographs of towns, cities, mountains, deserts, coasts, and archeological sites in more than one hundred countries. His pictures have revealed long-lost structures of ancient cultures, natural shifts in the landscape, the growth of cities, and changes in land cultivation.

Photo thoughts

 What problems do you think Gerster might encounter doing aerial photography?

How does this image suggest the enormity of the desert?

Why do you think Gerster took this particular picture?

Zoom In ▶

Gerster composed the image so that the road cuts diagonally across its center, cropping the camel caravan both front and back. This helps give a feeling of movement, as well as the sense of a long road.

"Altitude provides overview, overview provides insight, while insight eventually, I hope, leads to respect." —Georg Gerster

Sunflower No. 4 1991

Thomas Struth (German, b.1954)

The photograph

Struth was asked to take photographs to decorate patients' rooms in a new hospital in Switzerland. For each of the thirty-seven rooms, he photographed a different local landscape; each of these images included a path, leading through vineyards, forests, farmland, or gardens to a distant horizon. Struth also shot close-ups of familiar flowers with vibrant colors, such as this sunflower, as well as buds and twigs.

Large-scale landscape prints were hung on the wall opposite each bed, for the patient to enjoy. Two of the plant images, enlarged to poster size, were hung side by side behind each bed, cheering up visitors coming to see their sick relative or friend.

Blow Up

What difference do you notice between the foreground flower and the background?

The photographer

Struth is one of Germany's most famous art photographers. His large-scale works include family portraits, images of museum visitors looking at famous works of art, and shots of complex, contemporary technology and global development.

Photo thoughts

- 📷 Why do you think Struth chose to photograph views and plants of the local environment?
- 📷 Why might Struth have chosen to highlight single flowers, like this one?
- 📷 How might flower pictures in sick rooms influence patients' and visitors' experience of the hospital?

Zoom In ▶

The sunflower head was shot very close up, creating an intimate and powerful flower portrait. Every detail of its multi-colored pointy petals and swirly seed head is crisp, clear, and bright.

"[When] I am taking a photograph, I am conscious that I am constructing images rather than taking snapshots." —Thomas Struth

Ladybird Take-off 2007

Stephen Dalton (British, b. 1937)

The photograph

It convincingly appears that this photograph was taken in nature. In fact, Stephen Dalton built a "biologically truthful" arrangement on a tabletop. Here, he could direct insects to a specific spot and photograph them in mid-flight.

Since suitable equipment did not already exist for capturing movement at the right moment, Dalton spent two years creating his own photographic setup—developing his own light sensors, transformers, high-speed flash units, and homemade shutters.

Blow Up

Where do you think the light is coming from in this photograph? How can you tell?

The photographer

A pioneer in nature photography, Stephen Dalton was the first to capture pin-sharp images of insects in flight, with their fluttering wings frozen. He has shot other unusual photographs of animals in motion, such as leaping frogs, swooping birds, and ghostly owls, in controlled outdoor setups.

Photo thoughts

- What details of this ladybug might not be visible to the naked eye?
- How does having the plant stem help the composition of the photograph?
- How does this picture make you feel about nature?

Zoom In ▶

The ladybug looks as if it is about to land on a plant, but actually, it is taking off backwards! Dalton was able to make this sort of discovery thanks to his high-speed photographic system.

"The thrill of seeing for the first time how these little creatures moved their wings and maneuver through the air . . . was overwhelming." —Stephen Dalton

Io + Gatto (I + Cat) 1932

Wanda Wulz (Italian, 1903–1984)

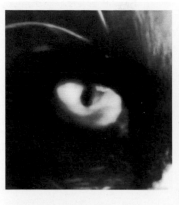

The photograph

The striking self-portrait of Wanda Wulz, an experimental Italian photographer, was created by a technique known as sandwich negatives. She took two separate pictures, one of herself and one of Pippo, her cat. In the darkroom, she put one negative on top of the other and printed a single merged image. In areas such as Wulz's neck and the right-hand side of her face, where her negative was thin (in deep shadow), details from the cat negative stand out most strongly. In areas such as Wulz's light fur collar and the left-hand side of her face, where her negative was denser (bright), details from the cat negative scarcely come through.

The photographer

Born into the third generation of a family of portrait photographers in Trieste, Italy, Wanda Wulz was taught by her father and ran her own portrait studio from 1928. She briefly joined the futurist movement and showed some of her experimental prints at their photographic exhibition.

Photo thoughts

- What elements of the photograph are of Wulz?
- What was the most important detail to line up in both photographs?
- Which, in your opinion, stands out more—the cat or Wulz? Or are they equal?

Blow Up

Can you distinguish the cat's eye from the photographer's eye?

Zoom In ▶

Some parts of the cat, such as its long whiskers, furry bib, wet nose, and white paw are clearly identifiable. Notice too the ghostly shapes of its pointed ears, which stick out on either side of Wulz's head.

© Wanda Wulz /Topfoto

"If man could be crossed with the cat it would improve man, but it would deteriorate the cat." —Mark Twain

Marilyn Diptych 1962

Andy Warhol (American, 1928–1987)

The photograph

Marilyn Monroe was the most famous film star of her time. Photographs of her appeared endlessly in magazines, newspapers, and publicity stills. After her death in 1962, Andy Warhol bought a publicity photograph of her, which he cropped, enlarged, and transferred onto a silk screen (a kind of stencil). He pressed black paint through the silk screen, creating an image identical to the original photograph. He duplicated the image fifty times, varying the amount of black paint to make either distinct, precise images or blurred, faded ones. He then printed half the faces in vivid, unreal colors, suggesting Marilyn Monroe's glamorous, but artificial, image in life. These contrast sharply with the black-and-white faces, reminding viewers of her death by suicide.

The photographer

Andy Warhol was obsessed with both fame and death. He made photographic silkscreen portraits of other famous people of the 1960s, including the singer Elvis Presley; Jacqueline Kennedy, widow of President Kennedy; and Mao Zedong, the leader of China.

Photo thoughts

- Why do you think Warhol duplicated Monroe's image so many times?
- Why do you think the black-and-white portraits become increasingly faded?
- Are these images still photographs?

Blow Up

Why do you think Warhol portrayed Monroe so heavily made up, with strong red lipstick and blue eye shadow?

Zoom In ▼

Warhol's mechanical way of repeating images raised questions about the role of the artist in creating art. It also challenged the idea that a portrait was unique and authentic only if it was hand-painted.

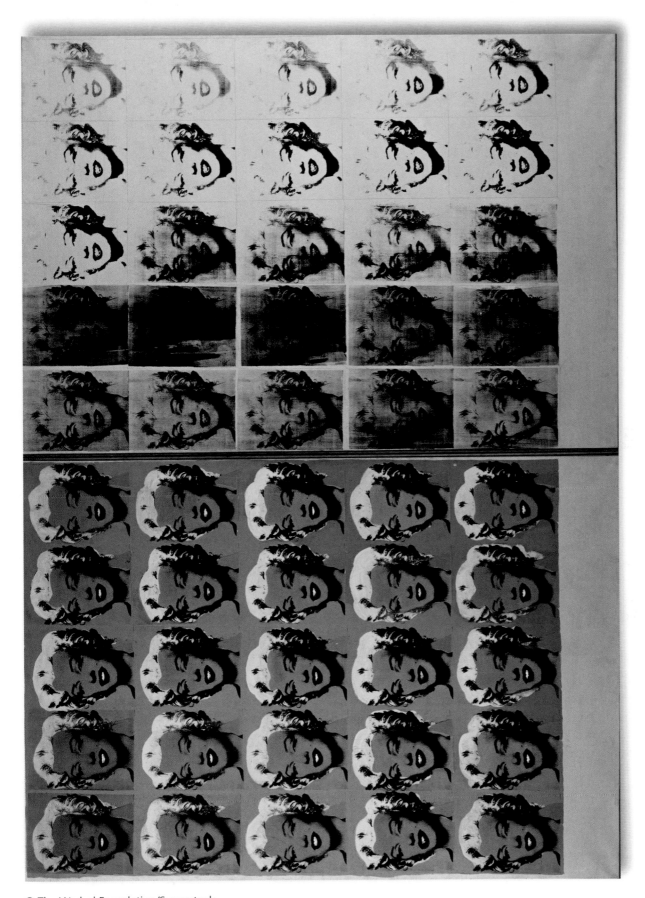

"In the future, everyone will be world-famous for fifteen minutes."

—Andy Warhol

Pearblossom Highway #2 1986

David Hockney (British, b. 1937)

The photograph

Measuring 6½ feet tall by 9 feet wide (almost 2 meters by 3 meters), this huge image of a California highway is a photographic collage that David Hockney calls a joiner. He built it up from hundreds of overlapping photos taken from different viewpoints over eight days. Hockney shot everything close up, to pull viewers into the picture. He photographed the road signs from up a ladder, the rubbish on the roadside from a ground-level crouch, and the trees and the horizon as he walked along the road. The final picture, with its multiple viewpoints and sharp details, shows a richer and more nuanced panoramic view than most wide-angle photographs could ever show. It is not, however, true to life. Hockney moved the signs closer together and chose where to position the large tree.

The photographer

Originally best known for his paintings, printmaking, and stage designs, David Hockney has made pictures with all sorts of technology, experimenting with photography, faxes, color copies, laser prints, and, most recently, with split-screen videos and the iPad.

Photo thoughts

◉ Can you see places in this image where Hockney has looked down on the road?
◎ How can you tell that Hockney photographed the road signs close up?
◎ What seems odd about the Pearblossom Highway sign?

Blow Up

How would a single photograph of a tree differ from this one made up of multiple shots?

Zoom In ▶

The image depicts the viewpoint of both driver and passenger. The right-hand side highlights signs drivers have to follow. The left-hand side draws the eye to details such as the roadside litter that passengers, with leisure to look around, might notice.

The J. Paul Getty Museum, Los Angeles. © 1986 David Hockney

"The picture is about driving without the car being in it." —David Hockney

99 Cent 1999

Andreas Gursky (German, b. 1955)

The photograph

Shot with a large-format wide-angle camera, Gursky's huge photographic print (almost 7 feet by 11 feet/2 meters by 3 meters) shows a downtown Los Angeles discount store. The apparently endless rows of tidy shelves are shot from a high viewpoint that shoppers would never have themselves. Gursky digitally manipulated the image to create an epic, perfect scene, overflowing with abundance and brightness. It gives us a strong sense of how the browsing shoppers might feel, confronted by such an overwhelming and excessive choice of mass-produced, colorfully packaged goods.

The photographer

Gursky is inspired by our contemporary, globalized world of large work spaces, stores, hotels, apartment buildings, and crowd-filled events. He makes the most of digital technology, piecing together multiple shots of an image to create detailed, panoramic, and, often, gridlike compositions. He also intensifies color and contrast. His prints are so enormous that they need to be viewed from a distance to see the whole composition, as well as close up to appreciate the sharply focused details.

Photo thoughts

- What do you think Gursky wanted us to think about when we view this image?
- What elements in this picture give it a sense of order and stillness? What breaks the order?
- What effect does Gursky achieve by making the colors so vivid?

Blow Up

What do you notice about the ceiling?

Zoom In ▶

Gursky has manipulated the image so that the horizontal shelves and upright columns form a grid with the goods in groups of repeating colors. Hold the book at arm's length and squint at the image. It will look almost as if it is an abstract pattern.

"I stand at a distance, like a person from another world."

—Andreas Gursky

The Cottingley Fairies 1917

Elsie Wright (British, 1901–1988)

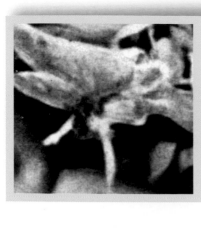

The photograph

In 1917, Frances Griffiths and Elsie Wright, young cousins living in Cottingley, a village in northern England, claimed they played with fairies in nearby woods. To prove it, Elsie borrowed a camera from her father. To his surprise, when he developed the photograph, this portrait of Frances with dancing fairies was revealed. In 1920, it came to the attention of Sir Arthur Conan Doyle, creator of the Sherlock Holmes books and a believer in spiritualism. He not only believed the photograph was genuine but also used it and others to illustrate articles and a book claiming that fairies existed. In 1983 Elsie Wright admitted that their fairy photographs were, in fact, hoaxes. She had drawn and painted the fairies on cardboard, cut them out, stuck them in place with hatpins, and then photographed them.

The photographer

Elsie Wright was sixteen when she took this photograph. She had some art training and probably copied the fairies from drawings in a book. The fairy photographs dogged her life, but as she later admitted, she was far too embarrassed to confess the truth about them after they had managed to fool such a prominent person as Conan Doyle.

Photo thoughts

- What do you think might have helped convince people that the fairies were real?
- What might make you think this photo was a hoax?
- How does the setting help add to the atmosphere of the photograph?

Blow Up

What difference do you notice between the lighting on Frances and on the fairies?

Zoom In ▼

Those who believed that the fairies were fake used the argument that their hairstyles seemed very modern — not something real fairies might be expected to concern themselves with!

"It was just Elsie and I having a bit of fun."

—Frances Griffiths

© Elsie Wright/Topfoto

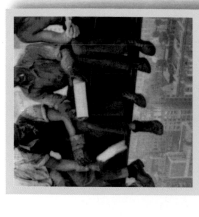

Blow Up

How did Ebbets dramatize the height of the beam on which the men are sitting?

Zoom In ▶

It seems incredible that the workers can seem so relaxed perched so high. They are chatting, smiling, eating, and holding lunch boxes. One is lighting another's cigarette, and another has an empty bottle in his hand.

Lunchtime atop a Skyscraper 1932

Charles C. Ebbets (American, 1905–1978)

The photograph

Skyscraper building boomed in New York City in the 1930s. Contractors took advantage of workers during the Great Depression, when unemployment reached 25 percent. Desperate men took perilous, low-paid construction jobs to support their families. Ebbets's breathtaking photograph celebrates these tough men, taking their lunch break on a crossbeam on the unfinished sixty-ninth floor of the RCA Building, part of Rockefeller Center. The ends of the beam are out of sight, so the men appear to float in the sky, high above any of the other tall buildings. Central Park stretches out on the right-hand side behind them.

The photographer

Ebbets was a fearless photographer who even risked taking aerial shots lying on the tail of a plane. He was also a daring hunter, pilot, wrestler, and race-car driver and explored unmapped areas of the Florida Everglades, photographing rare wildlife and the lives of the Seminole people who lived there.

Photo thoughts

- Where do you think the photographer was positioned to take this shot?
- What clues tell you that this was a staged publicity shot to promote this new skyscraper?
- Why is this photograph considered, as one critic put it, "an icon of American optimism and ingenuity"?

"Architecture is the will of an epoch translated into space."

—architect Ludwig Mies van der Rohe

Migrant Mother 1936

Dorothea Lange (American, 1895–1965)

The photograph

The Great Depression of the 1930s was marked by droughts that turned America's prairie farmland to parched dust. Thousands of poverty-struck families migrated to California, hoping to find work but ending up in squalid camps.

Lange's potent photograph of a hungry, destitute mother with her unkempt children pressed up against her at a pea pickers' camp has become an enduring image of the Depression. Published in the *San Francisco News,* the photograph spurred the federal government to send 20,000 pounds of food to Californian migrant workers.

The photographer

Dorothea Lange was one of a team of eleven photographers employed in 1935 by the Farm Security Administration to document the lives of migrant workers. Their photographs were used to publicize the devastating hardship of rural people.

Photo thoughts

- 📷 Lange asked the two older children to turn their heads for this photograph. Why might she have done this?
- 📷 Lange shot six pictures, starting at a distance, showing details of the family's makeshift tent and muddy fields, then coming closer. Why do you think the public found this close-up so shocking?
- 📷 What details in this picture show the family's poverty?

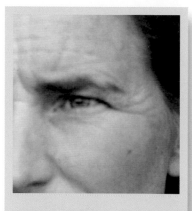

Blow Up

What adjectives would you use to describe the mother's expression?

Zoom In ▶

The tightly framed portrait focuses on the family, with the mother at the center. People in portraits usually look toward the camera, but here the mother gazes into the distance while two of her children look away and the baby is asleep.

"The camera is an instrument that teaches people how to see without a camera." —Dorothea Lange

Air-Raid Victim, London Blitz 1940

Cecil Beaton (British, 1904–1980)

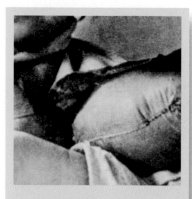

The photograph

During World War II, between September 1940 and May 1941, the German Luftwaffe (air force) repeatedly bombed British cities in a campaign known as the Blitz. Millions of houses were destroyed, and more than 200,000 civilians were killed or injured.

Three-year-old Eileen Dunne, one of the injured, was photographed in her hospital bed by Cecil Beaton. Featured on the cover of *Life* magazine, simply captioned "Air-Raid Victim," this poignant image of a suffering innocent summed up the random violence of war. It brought home to Americans the reality of the Blitz and the need to help Britain in its fight against Nazism.

The photographer

Best known for his stylish, elegant photographs of the rich and famous, Beaton was also a talented writer, painter, and illustrator. Commissioned by the Ministry of Information to document the war, Beaton took more than 7,000 photographs in China, Burma, and India, as well as in Britain.

Photo thoughts

◉ How far away did Beaton stand to take this photograph?

◉ How do you think Beaton wanted people to feel when they saw this picture?

◉ Do you think this is a more, or less, convincing image about the nature of war than one of injured soldiers?

Blow Up

How does the inclusion of Eileen's well-worn toy add to the atmosphere of the image?

Zoom In ▶

Beaton deliberately framed this shot to tug at people's heartstrings. Centrally positioned, framed by the bars of her bed, propped up by a big pillow, Eileen seems alone and vulnerable. She stares straight at the viewer, demanding our attention.

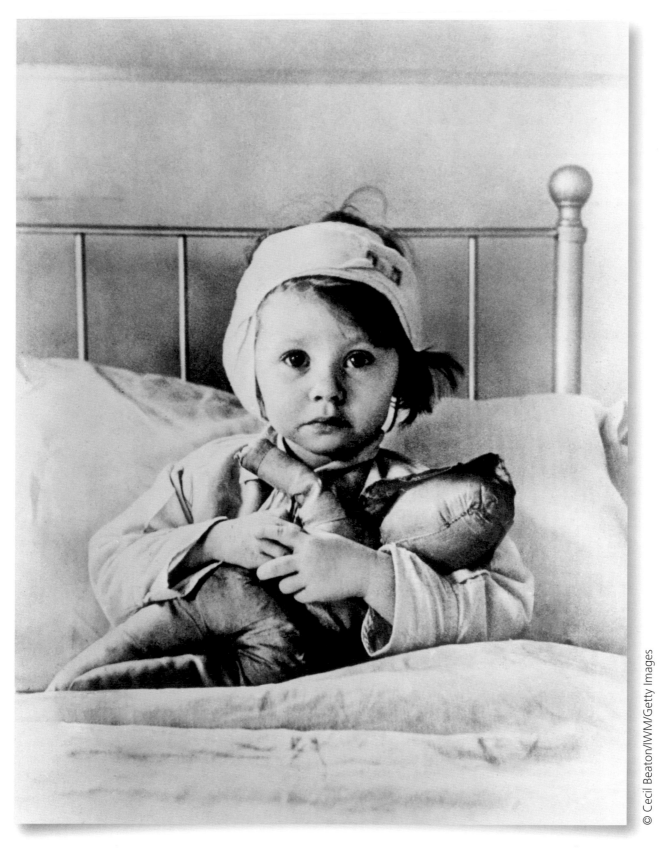

© Cecil Beaton/IWM/Getty Images

"Goering's attacks on London achieve little but the maiming and slaughtering of children."

—*Illustrated London News* caption, September 21, 1940

The Kiss by the Hôtel de Ville 1950

Robert Doisneau (French, 1912–1994)

The photograph

Considered one of the most romantic and popular photos ever taken, it has been reproduced on more than 500,000 posters and 400,000 postcards. The picture was taken for a photo spread about Paris lovers for *Life* magazine. The couple in the photo were believed to be two anonymous lovers caught unawares. Their identities remained a mystery until 1992, when a couple claiming to be the two in the shot took Doisneau to court for having taken their picture without their knowledge. This forced Doisneau to reveal that the shot had actually been staged. He had witnessed a different couple kissing in the street and had asked them to repeat it in various locations for his photograph.

The photographer

French photographer Robert Doisneau is largely known for his street photography. He captured playful, amusing images of different social classes in the streets of his hometown, Paris. He worked briefly as a fashion photographer for *Vogue* but found he didn't enjoy photographing beautiful women in elegant surroundings and left to continue photographing street culture.

Photo thoughts

- No one in the photo is looking at the couple. What does this add to the experience?
- What gives the image a sense of motion, as if it were caught quickly?
- Does the photo appear less romantic once you know that it was staged?

Blow Up

How does this passing woman make the photo feel more real?

Zoom In ▶

The only people in focus are the kissing couple and the woman just behind them. The apparently messy composition, with figures cropped on both sides, makes the photo appear as if the kiss were caught rather than posed.

"I don't photograph life as it is, but life as I would like it to be."

—Robert Doisneau

Muhammad Ali versus Sonny Liston 1965

Neil Leifer (American, b. 1942)

The photograph

Sports Illustrated magazine sent two photographers to cover the second world heavyweight boxing fight between Sonny Liston and Muhammad Ali (then known as Cassius Clay). Within a few minutes of the first round, Liston fell to the ground and lay prone, seemingly unable to get up. Leifer captured the dramatic instant when Ali stood over Liston, shouting, "Get up and fight, sucker!" The shot sums up the essence of Ali's force, confidence, and swagger. Eventually, Liston stood up and Ali knocked him out.

The photographer

An avid sports fan, Leifer has photographed many major sporting events, including numerous Olympic games, baseball world series, football Super Bowls, and heavyweight title fights. Boxing is his favorite sport, and he covered thirty of Muhammad Ali's fights.

Photo thoughts

- 📷 What is your impression of Muhammad Ali's character?
- 📷 How does the lighting contribute to the drama of the scene?
- 📷 Leifer has said, "What separates a great sports photographer from an ordinary one is that when they get lucky, they don't miss." What was lucky for Leifer with this shot?

Blow Up

What view would Herb Scharfman, the other *Sports Illustrated* photographer, have seen?

Zoom In ▶

Compare the bodies and gestures of the two boxers. Ali's arm and leg muscles are taut and prominent. His right arm is poised to lash out. Liston's body is floppy. Both arms are raised above his head, as if in a position of surrender.

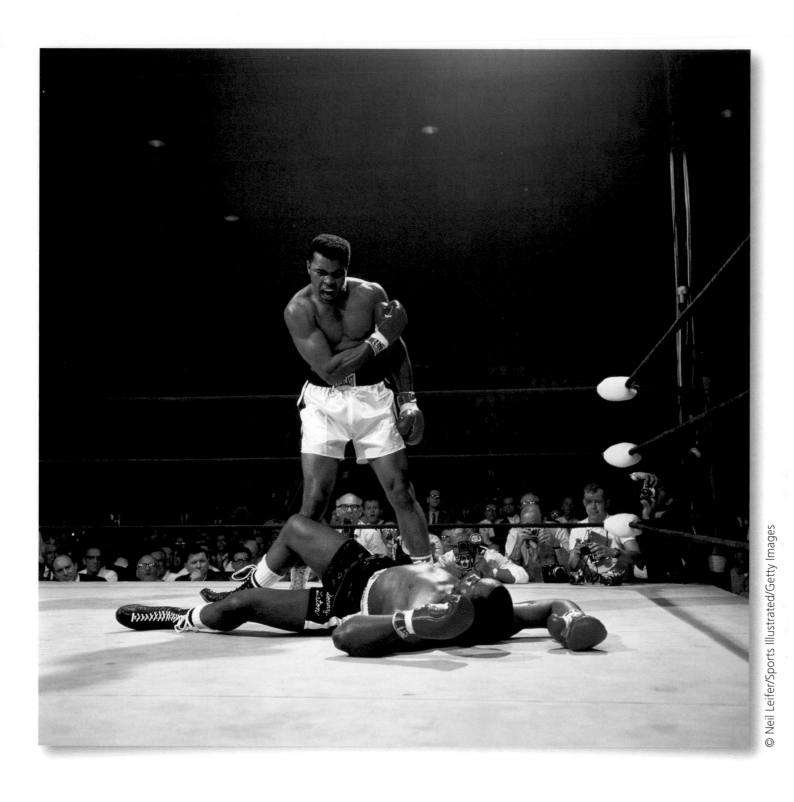

"When you're shooting ringside, you feel what the fighters feel." —Neil Leifer

Buzz Aldrin on the Moon 1969

Neil Armstrong (American, 1930–2012)

The photograph

Neil Armstrong took most of the photos from the *Apollo 11* mission, so there are not many images of him. In this picture he is reflected in Buzz Aldrin's visor, making it a double portrait.

An estimated 500 million people watched the moon landing on television, and Aldrin sees this image as embodying that moment when the world was brought together, with the reflection showing it to be a shared experience. However, there are some people who believe that the photos taken were all fakes and that they had been set up in a film studio. They question the high quality of the image and the fact that there are no stars visible in the sky.

The photographer

Known more for being the first man on the moon than for taking photos, Neil Armstrong was the main photographer of *Apollo 11*'s mission to the moon. He has received praise for the composition of his images, especially since he had no photographic training.

Photo thoughts

- 📷 Is this still a portrait of Buzz Aldrin, even though you cannot see his face?
- 📷 How does having the reflection of Neil Armstrong change the feeling of the photo?
- 📷 What might make someone think this photo was staged?

Blow Up

Aside from the photographer and the spacecraft, what else can you see in the reflection?

Zoom In ▶

We see an astronaut against the horizon of the moon with footprints and a piece of equipment in the foreground. Mirrored in the visor, that equipment is shown to be the spacecraft, and we can also see the photographer.

"In this one moment, the world came together in peace for all mankind." —Buzz Aldrin

Neil Armstrong/ NASA

New York City 1974

Elliott Erwitt (American, b. 1928)

The photograph

Does this photograph make you smile? This minute, forlorn Chihuahua would make an amusing image on its own, with its enormous ears and little legs, wearing a knitted coat and a ridiculous, oversize hat firmly knotted under its chin. What makes it much funnier is its juxtaposition with the shiny knee-high boots of its owner, who towers above it, and the front paws of a huge Great Dane, standing in an almost identical pose beside her. Shooting from the tiny dog's eye line, so that the rest of the owner and the back legs of the Great Dane are left out of the image, Erwitt created a comical shot that makes you look twice.

The photographer

Elliott Erwitt believes that you can find pictures anywhere. He has a keen eye for spotting comic and absurd moments in everyday life and capturing them with impeccable timing. He is skilled at composing his shots in the camera, rarely cropping or manipulating images afterward. He has frequently photographed dogs.

Photo thoughts

- How would this picture be different if it had been taken from farther away?
- Who is this picture about—the dogs or their owner? Why do you think this?
- What do you think of the title for this picture? What would you have titled it?

Blow Up

Where do you think the photographer positioned himself to take this view of the dog?

Zoom In ▶

The composition of this image is very precise. The vertical lines of legs, which fill the central portion of the image, are n sharp focus. These stand out boldy against the light, fuzzy background.

"To me, photography is the art of observing. It's about finding something interesting in an ordinary place.**"** —Elliott Erwitt

Serra Pelada Gold Mine 1986

Sebastião Salgado (Brazilian, b. 1944)

The photograph

An outstanding photojournalist, Salgado spent weeks documenting this mine in a remote part of Brazil, his home country. Gold had been discovered here some years earlier, attracting 50,000 hopeful prospectors. Some of his photographs, like this long shot, show the enormity of the man-made mine, with carved-out hollows and terraces and long, rickety ladders leaning against its steep sides. The packed crowd of miners, shifting their loads of earth, appear to move as one, in a continuous flow, like ants. By contrast, Salgado's close-ups focus on the strength and determination of individual miners, covered in mud, who clamber up slopes and ladders, every sinew straining.

The photographer

Salgado travels the world, for several years at a time, to take photographs on chosen themes. After photographing the gold miners, he went on to shoot other examples of hard physical labor in twenty-six countries, including shipbuilding in Poland, sulfur mining in Indonesia, sugarcane cutting in Cuba, and digging the Channel Tunnel in England.

Photo thoughts

- 📷 How does the absence of sky affect the atmosphere of this image?
- 📷 Why do you think Salgado prefers to shoot in black-and-white, rather than color?
- 📷 Why do you think Salgado called this image "a vision from the Middle Ages"? What is most obviously missing from it?

Blow Up

Does the mining look organized or chaotic? What makes you say that?

Zoom In ▶

Taken from a distance, this vertical image emphasizes the depth of the mine. Salgado's composition, with workers cropped off on all four sides, suggests that the mine stretches on and on, well beyond this frame.

"I'm a journalist. My life's on the road, my studio is the planet." —Sebastião Selgado

Tank Man 1989

Jeff Widener (American, b. 1956)

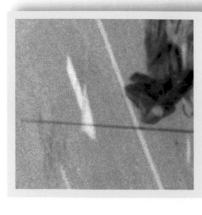

Blow Up

What do the arrows and lines on the road add to the power of the image?

The photograph

In June 1989, hundreds of thousands of students occupied Tiananmen Square in Beijing, China, to protest against government corruption and to demand freedom of speech and freedom of the press. The government ordered the People's Liberation Army to clear the square. They opened fire on the unarmed protesters, and there were many casualties.

Still banned in China more than twenty years after it was taken, this photograph of a lone man blocking a line of tanks on its way to Tiananmen Square has become an iconic image of this event.

The photographer

An experienced press photographer, Widener risked arrest to take this picture from a sixth-floor hotel balcony after the army had taken control. Thinking quickly, he enlisted the help of a passing American student who not only accompanied him, posing as a hotel guest, past security police into the hotel room, but also delivered Widener's film to the Associated Press office, hidden in his underwear.

Zoom In ▼

The tight view of a very wide road and the tanks shot on a diagonal help give this image much power. The lone man seems so vulnerable against these four huge machines, yet he has managed to stop them.

Photo thoughts

- The man is standing on a road crossing, holding two shopping bags. How do these details affect your view of the image?
- What does the inclusion of the street light add to the atmosphere of the photo?
- Why do you think this picture has become so iconic?

© Jeff Widener/AP/PAI

"I still think of him as the unknown soldier—the faceless guy who represents all of us." —Jeff Widener

Barcelona 2011

Martin Parr (British, b. 1952)

The photograph

Tourists throng to the Park Güell in Barcelona to see its quirky buildings and benches with intricate mosaics designed by the Catalan architect Antoni Gaudí. But, as Martin Parr's photograph wittily shows, contemporary tourists often spend their time taking photographs rather than simply meandering through this peaceful garden.

Parr has taken photographs at many famous tourist sites around the world. However, he is far more interested in capturing the way tourists behave and the guides, vendors, and signs around these sites than in the sites themselves.

The photographer

Parr is a documentary chronicler of contemporary everyday life, often with a humorous or ironic eye. He has become interested in the effects of globalization, consumerism, excessive wealth, and tourism. He is an avid collector of postcards, photography books, badges, and political ephemera, which he sometimes exhibits alongside his photos.

Photo thoughts

- Parr believes that "the act of photographing ourselves at tourist sites . . . makes us feel reassured that we are a part of the recognizable world." Do you agree with this view?
- When people used film, which was costly to buy and process, they took fewer photographs. What are the advantages and disadvantages of being able to take endless digital photographs?
- Do you think that taking photographs is the best way to hold on to an experience?

Blow Up

Is anyone in Parr's photograph looking at the site without holding a camera?

Zoom In ▶

This image supports Parr's claim that photography is the greatest democratic art form of our time. People of all ages have arranged themselves so they all get a good view, without other tourists in the way. Notice how some of them stand on a ledge.

© Martin Parr/Magnum Photos

"Now it is impossible for me to shoot a photograph where someone is *not* taking a picture or posing for one." —Martin Parr

Glossary

aerial photographs photographs taken from an airplane, helicopter, or hot-air balloon of land or sea below

background the part of a photo that appears farthest away from the viewer

close-up an image that shows a detail rather than the whole of a subject

commission the mechanism by which an individual or organization asks a photographer or other artist to produce work in exchange for a fee

composition the graphic arrangement of the elements of a photograph or other artwork

contrast the degree of difference between the darkest and lightest parts of a photograph or other artwork

cropping the process of cutting off an image at one or more edges, usually to improve its composition

depth of field the distance in a photograph from the closest point in focus to the most distant point still in focus

developing the chemical process by which an exposed photographic image is made visible

digital camera a camera that stores image data in digital format, which can be downloaded onto a computer and, if desired, manipulated

exposure the amount of light that is allowed to reach photographic film or an image sensor

flash unit an instrument that creates a bright, brief artificial burst of light to illuminate a dark scene when a photograph is being taken

foreground the part of a photograph that appears closest to the viewer

frame the process by which a photographer chooses which parts of a view will fall within the boundaries of a photograph

futurism an artistic movement that started in Italy in about 1910. Its artists were inspired by, and tried to express, the dynamism of contemporary life and the speed and force of modern machinery.

grid a network of vertical and horizontal lines spaced uniformly

horizon the line where the land or sea meets the sky

juxtaposition the placement of two or more things side by side

large-format camera a camera that uses film that is 4 x 5 inches (10 x 13 centimeters) or larger; often used for landscape photography

negative photographic film that has been exposed to light, in which the light parts appear dark and the dark parts appear light. A negative is used for making a photographic print.

panorama a wide view in all directions, often of a large area of land or a city

photojournalist someone who tells a news story through photographs, often with added text

point of view the angle from which a viewer or photographer sees a person, object, or scene

portrait an image of a particular person or group of people

pose the deliberate positioning of someone's head, body, arms, and legs

shutter the part of a camera that opens and closes to let light through for a certain length of time

silhouette an outline filled with shadow, showing the shape of a person or thing against a light background

strobe a lamp that produces very short and intense light flashes

tone the quality of light or darkness in a photograph

viewpoint the position, angle, and direction from which a photographer takes a picture

wide-angle lens a lens that provides a wider view than standard lenses

zoopraxiscope a device that projects discs of still images in rapid succession, giving an impression of movement

Index

Adams, Ansel 18–19
Afghan Girl 10–11
Afghanistan 10–11
Air-Raid Victim, London Blitz 42–43
Aldrin, Buzz 48–49
Ali, Muhammad 46–47
Anders, William 20–21
Apollo 8 20
Apollo 11 48–49
Armstrong, Neil 48–49

Baracoa (Cuba) 14–15
Barcelona 56–57
Beaton, Cecil 42–43
Blitz, the 42–43
boxing 46–47
Brazil 52–53
Burnand, Hugo 12–13
Buzz Aldrin on the Moon 48–49

California 32–33, 40–41
Camel Caravan 22–23
Castro, Fidel 8
China 30, 54–55
Conan Doyle, Sir Arthur 36
Cottingley Fairies, The 3, 36–37
Cuba 8–9, 14–15, 52

Daguerre, Louis 4–5
daguerreotypes 4–5
Dalton, Stephen 26–27
dogs 50–51
Doisneau, Robert 3, 44–45
Dunne, Eileen 42–43

Earthrise 20–21
Ebbets, Charles C. 38–39
England 12–13, 36–37, 42–43
Erwitt, Elliott 50–51

Family, British Royal 12–13

Gaudí, Antoni 56
Gerster, Georg 22–23

Great Depression, the 38, 40
Griffiths, Frances 36–37
Guevara, Che 8–9
Gula, Sharbat 10–11
Gursky, Andreas 34–35
Gutiérrez, Alberto Diaz 8–9

Heroic Guerrilla Fighter 8–9
Hockney, David 3, 32–33
Horse in Motion, The 16–17

Illustrated London News 45
Io + Gatto (I + Cat) 28–29
Iran 22–23

Kiss by the Hôtel de Ville, The 44–45
Korda, Alberto 8–9

Ladybird Take-off 26–27
Lange, Dorothea 40–41
Leifer, Neil 46–47
Life magazine 6, 42, 44
Liston, Sonny 46–47
Lunchtime atop a Skyscraper 38–39

Marilyn Diptych 30–31
McCurry, Steve 10–11
Meily Mendoza Singing to Her Doll 14–15
Middleton, Kate 12–13
Migrant Mother 40–41
Mili, Gjon 6–7
miners, gold 52–53
Monroe, Marilyn 30–31
moon, the 20–21, 48–49
Muhammad Ali versus Sonny Liston 46–47
Muybridge, Eadweard 16–17

National Geographic 10
negatives, sandwiching 28–29
New York City 38–39, 50–51
New York City (photo) 50–51
99 Cent 34–35

Paris 44–45
Parr, Martin 56–57
Pearblossom Highway #2 32–33

photography,
    aerial 22–23
    art 3, 28–35
    documentary 3, 36–57
    hoax 3, 36–37
    landscape 18–19, 24, 32–33
    nature 2, 16–27
    portrait 2, 4–15, 24, 28–29, 30–31, 40–41, 42–43, 48–49
    sports 46–47
photojournalists 3, 10, 52, 54
Picasso, Pablo 6–7
Prince William 12–13

refugees 10–11
Revolution, Cuban 8
Rodero, Cristina Garcia 14–15
Rohe, Ludwig Mies van der 39
Royal Wedding 12–13

Sabatier-Blot, Jean-Baptiste 4
Salgado, Sebastião 52–53
San Francisco News 40
Scharfman, Herb 46
Serra Pelada Gold Mine 52–53
shutter speed 6, 16, 18, 26
Sontag, Susan 17
space 20–21, 48–49
Sports Illustrated 46
Stanford, Leland 16
Struth, Thomas 24–25
Sunflower No. 4 24–25

Tank Man 54–55
The Tetons and the Snake River, The 18–19
Tiananmen Square 54–55
tourism 3, 56–57
Twain, Mark 29

war 3, 8, 10, 42–43
Warhol, Andy 3, 30–31
Widener, Jeff 54–55
World War II 42
Wright, Elsie 36–37
Wulz, Wanda 28–29

zoopraxiscope 16